This journal belongs to

_____

BIBLE PROMISES

for Women

JOURNAL

Belle City Gifts
Racine, Wisconsin, USA

Belle City Gifts is an imprint of BroadStreet Publishing Group LLC.
Broadstreetpublishing.com

Bible Promises for Women Journal
© 2015 by BroadStreet Publishing

ISBN 978-1-4245-5150-7

Cover and interior design by Garborg Design Works | www.garborgdesign.com
Compiled and edited by Michelle Winger | www.literallyprecise.com

Printed in China.

15   16   17   18   19   20   21   7   6   5   4   3   2   1

Introduction

The world is a hectic place. Multiply that
exponentially and you have a woman's world.

If you take just a few moments to sit and
write, while pondering the inspirational
Scripture found on each page of this journal,
you can find the grace, peace, hope, and joy
you need to get through your day.

Be encouraged and strengthened as you
reflect on God's Word. His promises are
steady and true.

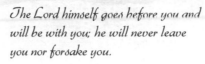

The Lord himself goes before you and will be with you; he will never leave you nor forsake you.

DEUTERONOMY 31:8 NIV

The Lord loves justice and fairness; he will never
abandon his people. They will be kept safe forever.

PSALM 37:28 TLB

You, God, see the trouble of the afflicted;
you consider their grief and take it in hand.
The victims commit themselves to you;
you are the helper of the fatherless.

PSALM 10:14 NIV

The LORD hears his people when they call to him for help.
He rescues them from all their troubles.

PSALM 34:17 NLT

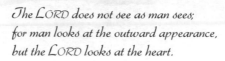

The LORD does not see as man sees;
for man looks at the outward appearance,
but the LORD looks at the heart.

1 SAMUEL 16:7 NKJV

If God is for us, who can be against us?

ROMANS 8:31 ESV

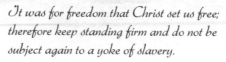

It was for freedom that Christ set us free;
therefore keep standing firm and do not be
subject again to a yoke of slavery.

GALATIANS 5:1 NASB

Submit to God. Resist the devil and he will flee from you,

JAMES 4:7 NKJV

Everyone should be quick to listen,
slow to speak and slow to become angry,
because human anger does not produce
the righteousness that God desires.

JAMES 1:19-20 NIV

_____

_____

_____

_____

_____

_____

_____

_____

_____

_____

_____

_____

_____

_____

_____

_____

_____

_____

_____

_____

_____

_____

_____

_____

_____

_____

_____

_____

_____

_____

_____

_____

_____

_____

_____

_____

_____

_____

Those with good sense are slow to anger,
and it is their glory to overlook an offense.

PROVERBS 19:11 NRSV

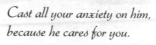

Cast all your anxiety on him,
because he cares for you.

1 PETER 5:7 NRSV

You keep him in perfect peace
whose mind is stayed on you,
because he trusts in you.

ISAIAH 26:3 ESV

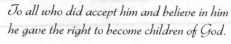

*To all who did accept him and believe in him
he gave the right to become children of God.*

JOHN 1:12 NCV

_____

_____

_____

_____

_____

_____

_____

_____

_____

_____

_____

_____

_____

_____

_____

_____

_____

_____

_____

_____

_____

"Blessed are those who have not seen and yet have believed."

JOHN 20:29 ESV

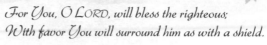

For You, O LORD, will bless the righteous;
With favor You will surround him as with a shield.

PSALM 5:12 NKJV

Surely you have granted him unending blessings
and made him glad with the joy of your presence.

PSALM 21:6 NIV

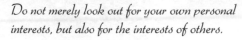

Do not merely look out for your own personal interests, but also for the interests of others.

PHILIPPIANS 2:4 NASB

Religion that is pure and undefiled before God, the Father,
is this: to care for orphans and widows in their distress,
and to keep oneself unstained by the world.

JAMES 1:27 NRSV

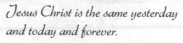

*Jesus Christ is the same yesterday
and today and forever.*

HEBREWS 13:8 NASB

_____

_____

_____

_____

_____

_____

_____

_____

_____

_____

_____

_____

_____

_____

_____

_____

_____

_____

_____

_____

Every good gift and every perfect gift is from above,
coming down from the Father of lights with whom
there is no variation or shadow due to change.

JAMES 1:17 ESV

Commit your work to the LORD,
and your plans will be established.

PROVERBS 16:3 ESV

_____

_____

_____

_____

_____

_____

_____

_____

_____

_____

_____

_____

_____

_____

_____

_____

_____

_____

_____

_____

_____

"Seek first the kingdom of God and His righteousness,
and all these things shall be added to you."

MATTHEW 6:33 NKJV

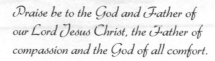

Praise be to the God and Father of our Lord Jesus Christ, the Father of compassion and the God of all comfort.

2 CORINTHIANS 1:3 NIV

_____

_____

_____

_____

_____

_____

_____

_____

_____

_____

_____

_____

_____

_____

_____

_____

_____

_____

_____

_____

_____

_____

_____

_____

_____

_____

_____

_____

_____

_____

_____

_____

_____

_____

_____

_____

_____

_____

_____

Yet the LORD longs to be gracious to you;
Therefore he will rise up to show you compassion.
For the LORD is a God of justice.
Blessed are all who wait for him!

ISAIAH 30:18 NIV

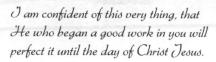

*I am confident of this very thing, that
He who began a good work in you will
perfect it until the day of Christ Jesus.*

PHILIPPIANS 1:6 NASB

_____

_____

_____

_____

_____

_____

_____

_____

_____

_____

_____

_____

_____

_____

_____

_____

_____

_____

_____

_____

_____

_____

_____

I can do everything through Christ, who gives me strength.

PHILIPPIANS 4:13 NLT

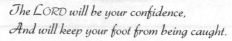

The LORD will be your confidence,
And will keep your foot from being caught.

PROVERBS 3:26 NKJV

_____

_____

_____

_____

_____

_____

_____

_____

_____

_____

_____

_____

_____

_____

_____

_____

Let us then approach God's throne of grace with confidence, so that we may receive mercy and find grace to help us in our time of need.

HEBREWS 4:16 NIV

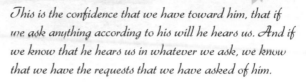

This is the confidence that we have toward him, that if we ask anything according to his will he hears us. And if we know that he hears us in whatever we ask, we know that we have the requests that we have asked of him.

1 JOHN 5:14 ESV

_____

_____

_____

_____

_____

_____

_____

_____

_____

_____

_____

_____

_____

_____

_____

_____

_____

_____

_____

_____

_____

_____

_____

For we are God's masterpiece. He has created
us anew in Christ Jesus, so we can do the good
things he planned for us long ago.

EPHESIANS 2:10 NLT

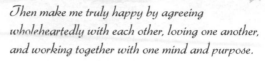

Then make me truly happy by agreeing wholeheartedly with each other, loving one another, and working together with one mind and purpose.

PHILIPPIANS 2:2 NLT

Be of the same mind toward one another. Do not
set your mind on high things, but associate with the
humble. Do not be wise in your own opinion.

ROMANS 12:16 NKJV

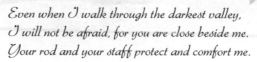

Even when I walk through the darkest valley,
I will not be afraid, for you are close beside me.
Your rod and your staff protect and comfort me.

PSALM 23:4 NLT

Be strong and courageous. Do not be frightened,
and do not be dismayed, for the LORD your God
is with you wherever you go.

JOSHUA 1:9 ESV

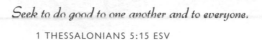

Seek to do good to one another and to everyone.

1 THESSALONIANS 5:15 ESV

Let your speech always be with grace, as though
seasoned with salt, so that you will know how
you should respond to each person.

COLOSSIANS 4:6 NASB

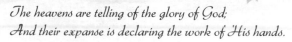

The heavens are telling of the glory of God;
And their expanse is declaring the work of His hands.

PSALM 19:1 NASB

_____

_____

_____

_____

_____

_____

_____

_____

_____

_____

_____

_____

_____

_____

The whole earth is filled with awe at your wonders.

PSALM 65:8 NIV

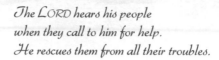

The LORD hears his people
when they call to him for help.
He rescues them from all their troubles.

PSALM 34:17 NLT

Why am I so sad?
Why am I so upset?
I should put my hope in God
and keep praising him.

PSALM 42:11 NCV

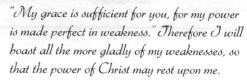

"My grace is sufficient for you, for my power is made perfect in weakness." Therefore I will boast all the more gladly of my weaknesses, so that the power of Christ may rest upon me.

2 CORINTHIANS 12:9 ESV

Take a new grip with your tired hands and strengthen your
weak knees. Mark out a straight path for your feet so that
those who are weak and lame will not fall but become strong.

HEBREWS 12:12-14 NLT

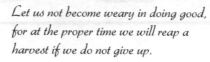

*Let us not become weary in doing good,
for at the proper time we will reap a
harvest if we do not give up.*

GALATIANS 6:9 NIV

Let us not neglect our meeting together, as some
people do, but encourage one another, especially
now that the day of his return is drawing near.

HEBREWS 10:25 NLT

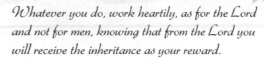

Whatever you do, work heartily, as for the Lord and not for men, knowing that from the Lord you will receive the inheritance as your reward.

COLOSSIANS 3:23-24 ESV

_____

_____

_____

_____

_____

_____

_____

_____

_____

_____

_____

_____

_____

_____

_____

_____

_____

_____

_____

_____

_____

_____

Do your best to present yourself to God as one
approved by him, a worker who has no need to be
ashamed, rightly explaining the word of truth.

2 TIMOTHY 2:15 NRSV

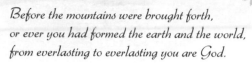

Before the mountains were brought forth,
or ever you had formed the earth and the world,
from everlasting to everlasting you are God.

PSALM 90:2 ESV

_____

_____

_____

_____

_____

_____

_____

_____

_____

_____

_____

_____

_____

_____

_____

_____

_____

_____

_____

_____

_____

"I will come back and take you to be with me
that you also may be where I am."

JOHN 14:3 NIV

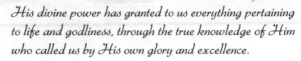

His divine power has granted to us everything pertaining to life and godliness, through the true knowledge of Him who called us by His own glory and excellence.

2 PETER 1:3 NASB

"If you have faith like a grain of mustard seed, you will
say to this mountain, 'Move from here to there,' and
it will move, and nothing will be impossible for you."

MATTHEW 17:20 ESV

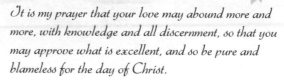

It is my prayer that your love may abound more and more, with knowledge and all discernment, so that you may approve what is excellent, and so be pure and blameless for the day of Christ.

PHILIPPIANS 1:9-10 ESV

Therefore, whether you eat or drink,
or whatever you do, do all to the glory of God.

1 CORINTHIANS 10:31 NKJV

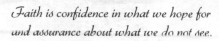

*Faith is confidence in what we hope for
and assurance about what we do not see.*

HEBREWS 11:1 NIV

Without faith it is impossible to please God, because anyone who comes to him must believe that he exists and that he rewards those who earnestly seek him.

HEBREWS 11:6 NIV

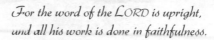

For the word of the LORD is upright,
and all his work is done in faithfulness.

PSALM 33:4 ESV

_____

_____

_____

_____

_____

_____

_____

_____

_____

_____

_____

_____

_____

_____

_____

_____

_____

_____

_____

_____

_____

_____

_____

_____

_____

_____

_____

_____

_____

_____

_____

_____

_____

_____

_____

_____

_____

_____

God is faithful. He will not allow the temptation to be
more than you can stand. When you are tempted,
he will show you a way out so that you can endure.

1 CORINTHIANS 10:13 NLT

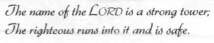

The name of the LORD is a strong tower;
The righteous runs into it and is safe.

PROVERBS 18:10 NASB

_____

_____

_____

_____

_____

_____

_____

_____

_____

_____

_____

_____

_____

_____

_____

_____

When you lie down, you will not be afraid;
when you lie down, your sleep will be sweet.

PROVERBS 3:24 NIV

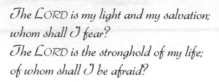

The LORD is my light and my salvation;
whom shall I fear?
The LORD is the stronghold of my life;
of whom shall I be afraid?

PSALM 27:1 ESV

_____

_____

_____

_____

_____

_____

_____

_____

_____

_____

_____

_____

_____

_____

_____

_____

_____

_____

_____

_____

_____

For God has not given us a spirit of fear,
but of power and of love and of a sound mind.

2 TIMOTHY 1:7 NKJV

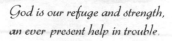

God is our refuge and strength,
an ever present help in trouble.

PSALM 46:1-3 NIV

_____

_____

_____

_____

_____

_____

_____

_____

_____

_____

_____

_____

_____

_____

_____

_____

_____

_____

But now, O LORD,
You are our Father;
We are the clay, and You our potter;
And all we are the work of Your hand.

ISAIAH 64:8 NKJV

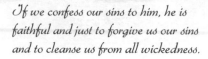

*If we confess our sins to him, he is
faithful and just to forgive us our sins
and to cleanse us from all wickedness.*

1 JOHN 1:9 NLT

He is so rich in kindness and grace that he
purchased our freedom with the blood of
his Son and forgave our sins.

EPHESIANS 1:7 NLT

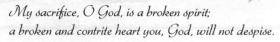

My sacrifice, O God, is a broken spirit;
a broken and contrite heart you, God, will not despise.

PSALM 51:17 NIV

For You, Lord, are good, and ready to forgive,
And abundant in mercy to all those who call upon You.

PSALM 86:5 NKJV

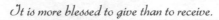

It is more blessed to give than to receive.

ACTS 20:35 NIV

Whoever is generous to the poor lends to the Lord,
and he will repay him for his deed.

PROVERBS 19:17 ESV

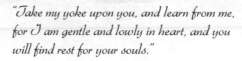

"Take my yoke upon you, and learn from me, for I am gentle and lowly in heart, and you will find rest for your souls."

MATTHEW 11:29-30 ESV

_____

_____

_____

_____

_____

_____

_____

_____

_____

_____

_____

_____

_____

_____

_____

_____

_____

Blessed are the gentle, for they shall inherit the earth

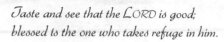

Taste and see that the LORD is good;
blessed is the one who takes refuge in him.

PSALM 34:8 NIV

_____

_____

_____

_____

_____

_____

_____

_____

_____

_____

_____

_____

_____

_____

_____

_____

_____

_____

_____
_____
_____
_____
_____
_____
_____
_____
_____
_____
_____
_____
_____
_____
_____
_____
_____
_____
_____
_____
_____
_____

The LORD is good to all,
and his mercy is over all that he has made.

PSALM 145:9 ESV

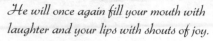

He will once again fill your mouth with
laughter and your lips with shouts of joy.

JOB 8:21 NLT

The ransomed of the LORD will return. They will enter Zion with
singing; everlasting joy will crown their heads. Gladness and joy will
overtake them, and sorrow and sighing will flee away.

ISAIAH 35:10 NIV

To all who mourn in Israel he will give: beauty for ashes; joy instead of mourning; praise instead of heaviness. For God has planted them like strong and graceful oaks for his own glory.

ISAIAH 61:3 TLB

I consider that the sufferings of this present time are not worth
comparing with the glory that is to be revealed to us.

ROMANS 8:18 ESV

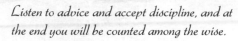

*Listen to advice and accept discipline, and at
the end you will be counted among the wise.*

PROVERBS 19:20 NIV

We can make our plans, but the Lord determines our steps.

PROVERBS 16:9 NLT

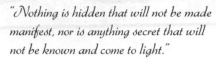

"Nothing is hidden that will not be made manifest, nor is anything secret that will not be known and come to light."

LUKE 8:17 ESV

Those who deal truthfully are His delight.

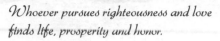

*Whoever pursues righteousness and love
finds life, prosperity and honor.*

PROVERBS 21:21 NIV

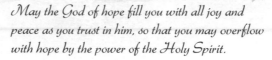

May the God of hope fill you with all joy and peace as you trust in him, so that you may overflow with hope by the power of the Holy Spirit.

ROMANS 15:13 NIV

The LORD takes pleasure in those who fear Him,
In those who hope in His mercy.

PSALM 147:11 NKJV

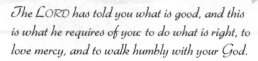

The LORD has told you what is good, and this is what he requires of you: to do what is right, to love mercy, and to walk humbly with your God.

MICAH 6:8 NLT

Pride will ruin people,

but those who are humble will be honored.

PROVERBS 29:23 NCV

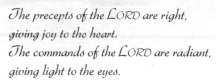

The precepts of the LORD are right,
giving joy to the heart.
The commands of the LORD are radiant,
giving light to the eyes.

PSALM 19:8 NIV

Your laws are my treasure;
they are my heart's delight.

PSALM 119:111 NLT

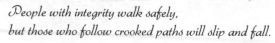

People with integrity walk safely,
but those who follow crooked paths will slip and fall.

PROVERBS 10:9 NLT

Because of my integrity, you uphold me
and set me in your presence forever.

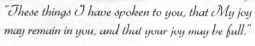

"These things I have spoken to you, that My joy
may remain in you, and that your joy may be full."

JOHN 15:11 NKJV

_____

_____

_____

_____

_____

_____

_____

_____

_____

_____

_____

_____

_____

_____

_____

_____

You will go out with joy and be led out in peace.
The mountains and hills will burst into song before you,
and all the trees in the fields will clap their hands.

ISAIAH 55:12 NCV

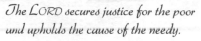

*The LORD secures justice for the poor
and upholds the cause of the needy.*

PSALM 140:12 NIV

_____

_____

_____

_____

_____

_____

_____

_____

_____

_____

_____

_____

_____

_____

_____

_____

Righteousness and justice are the foundation of your throne.

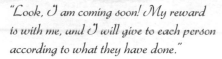

"Look, I am coming soon! My reward is with me, and I will give to each person according to what they have done."

REV 22:12 NIV

_____

_____

_____

_____

_____

_____

_____

_____

_____

_____

_____

_____

_____

_____

_____

_____

_____

The LORD is coming to judge the earth.
He will judge the world with justice,
and the nations with fairness.

PSALM 98:9 NLT

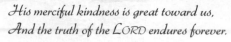

His merciful kindness is great toward us,
And the truth of the LORD endures forever.

PSALM 117:2 NKJV

_____

_____

_____

_____

_____

_____

_____

_____

_____

_____

_____

_____

_____

_____

_____

_____

_____

_____

_____

_____

_____

_____

"Love your enemies, and do good, and lend,
expecting nothing in return, and your reward will
be great, and you will be sons of the Most High."

LUKE 6:35 ESV

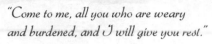

*"Come to me, all you who are weary
and burdened, and I will give you rest."*

MATTHEW 11:28 NIV

_____

_____

_____

_____

_____

_____

_____

_____

_____

_____

_____

_____

_____

_____

_____

_____

_____

_____

_____

_____

Satisfy us in the morning with your unfailing love,
that we may sing for joy and be glad all our days.

PSALM 90:14 NIV

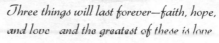

Three things will last forever—faith, hope,
and love and the greatest of these is love

1 CORINTHIANS 13:13 NLT

They who wait for the Lord shall renew their strength;
they shall mount up with wings like eagles;
they shall run and not be weary;
they shall walk and not faint.

ISAIAH 40:31 ESV

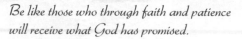

*Be like those who through faith and patience
will receive what God has promised.*

HEBREWS 6:12 NCV

I wait for the LORD, my whole being waits,
and in his word I put my hope.

PSALM 130:5 NIV

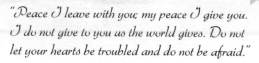

"Peace I leave with you; my peace I give you. I do not give to you as the world gives. Do not let your hearts be troubled and do not be afraid."

JOHN 14:27 NIV

_____

_____

_____

_____

_____

_____

_____

_____

_____

_____

_____

_____

_____

_____

_____

The LORD will give strength to his people;
The LORD will bless his people with peace.

PSALM 29:11 NKJV

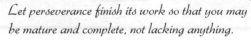

*Let perseverance finish its work so that you may
be mature and complete, not lacking anything.*

JAMES 1:4 NIV

Blessed is anyone who endures temptation. Such a one
has stood the test and will receive the crown of life that
the Lord has promised to those who love him.

JAMES 1:12 NRSV

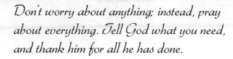

Don't worry about anything; instead, pray about everything. Tell God what you need, and thank him for all he has done.

PHILIPPIANS 4:6 NLT

My voice You shall hear in the morning, O Lord;
In the morning I will direct it to You,
And I will look up.

PSALM 5:3 NKJV

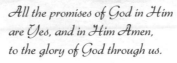

All the promises of God in Him
are Yes, and in Him Amen,
to the glory of God through us.

2 CORINTHIANS 1:20 NKJV

The LORD always keeps his promises;
he is gracious in all he does.

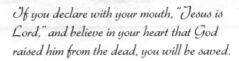

If you declare with your mouth, "Jesus is Lord," and believe in your heart that God raised him from the dead, you will be saved.

ROMANS 10:9 NIV

_____

_____

_____

_____

_____

_____

_____

_____

_____

_____

_____

_____

_____

_____

_____

_____

_____

_____

_____

_____

_____

_____

_____

_____

_____

_____

_____

_____

_____

_____

_____

_____

_____

_____

_____

_____

Your promises have been thoroughly tested,
and your servant loves them.

PSALM 119:40 NIV

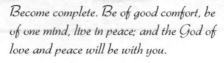

Become complete. Be of good comfort, be of one mind, live in peace; and the God of love and peace will be with you.

2 CORINTHIANS 13:11 NKJV

_____

_____

_____

_____

_____

_____

_____

_____

_____

_____

_____

_____

_____

_____

_____

_____

_____

_____

_____

_____

_____

_____

The desires of the diligent are fully satisfied.

PROVERBS 13:4 NIV

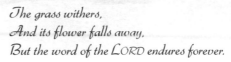

The grass withers,
And its flower falls away,
But the word of the LORD endures forever.

1 PETER 1:24-25 NKJV

_____

_____

_____

_____

_____

_____

_____

_____

_____

_____

_____

_____

_____

_____

_____

_____

_____

_____

_____

_____

_____

_____

_____

_____

_____

_____

_____

_____

_____

_____

_____

_____

_____

_____

He will give eternal life to those who keep on doing good,
seeking after the glory and honor and immortality that God offers.

ROMANS 2:7 NLT

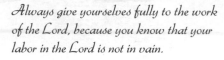

Always give yourselves fully to the work of the Lord, because you know that your labor in the Lord is not in vain.

1 CORINTHIANS 15:58 NIV

My flesh and my heart may fail,
but God is the strength of my heart
and my portion forever.

PSALM 73:26 NIV

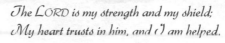

The LORD is my strength and my shield;
My heart trusts in him, and I am helped.

PSALM 28:7 NASB

_____
_____
_____
_____
_____
_____
_____
_____
_____
_____
_____
_____
_____
_____
_____

But for you who fear my name,
the sun of righteousness shall rise
with healing in its wings.

Commit your actions to the LORD.
and your plans will succeed.

PROVERBS 16:3 NLT

Those who know Your name will put their trust in You;
For You, LORD, have not forsaken those who seek You.

PSALM 9:10 NKJV

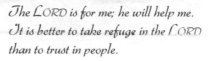

The LORD is for me; he will help me.
It is better to take refuge in the LORD
than to trust in people.

PSALM 118:7-8 NLT

I trust in you, O LORD;
I say, "You are my God."
My times are in your hand.

PSALM 31:14-15 ESV

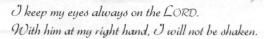

*I keep my eyes always on the LORD.
With him at my right hand, I will not be shaken.*

PSALM 16:8 NIV

_____

_____

_____

_____

_____

_____

_____

_____

_____

_____

_____

_____

_____

_____

_____

_____

The law of the LORD is perfect,
refreshing the soul.

PSALM 19:7 NIV

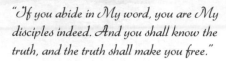

"If you abide in My word, you are My disciples indeed. And you shall know the truth, and the truth shall make you free."

JOHN 8:31-32 NKJV

_____

_____

_____

_____

_____

_____

_____

_____

_____

_____

_____

_____

_____

_____

_____

_____

You were cleansed from your sins when you obeyed the truth.

1 PETER 1:22 NLT

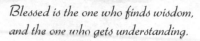

Blessed is the one who finds wisdom,
and the one who gets understanding.

PROVERBS 3:13 ESV

Do not let wisdom and understanding out of your sight,
preserve sound judgment and discretion;
they will be life for you.

PROVERBS 3:21-22 NIV

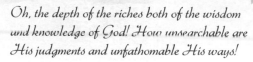

Oh, the depth of the riches both of the wisdom and knowledge of God! How unsearchable are His judgments and unfathomable His ways!

ROMANS 11:33 NASB

The LORD gives wisdom;
from his mouth come knowledge and understanding.

PROVERBS 2:6-7 ESV

If any of you lacks wisdom, you should ask God, who gives generously to all without finding fault, and it will be given to you.

JAMES 1:5 NIV

_____

_____

_____

_____

_____

_____

_____

_____

_____

_____

_____

_____

_____

_____

_____

_____

The wisdom from above is first of all pure. It is also peace loving, gentle at all times, and willing to yield to others. It is full of mercy and good deeds. It shows no favoritism and is always sincere.

JAMES 3:17 NLT

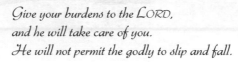

Give your burdens to the LORD,
and he will take care of you.
He will not permit the godly to slip and fall.

PSALM 55:22 NLT

You will experience God's peace, which exceeds anything we can understand. His peace will guard your hearts and minds as you live in Christ Jesus.

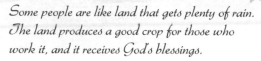

Some people are like land that gets plenty of rain.
The land produces a good crop for those who
work it, and it receives God's blessings.

HEBREWS 6:7 NCV

_____

_____

_____

_____

_____

_____

_____

_____

_____

_____

_____

_____

_____

_____

_____

_____

_____

_____

_____

_____

He who has clean hands and a pure heart,
Who has not lifted up his soul to falsehood
And has not sworn deceitfully.
He shall receive a blessing from the Lord
And righteousness from the God of his salvation.

PSALM 24:5 NASB